Jilted City

PATRICK MCGUINNESS was born in 1968 in Tunisia of Belgian and Newcastle Irish family, and now lives in Caernarfon, North Wales. He won an Eric Gregory Award for Poetry in 1998, the Levinson Prize from *Poetry* (Chicago) and the Poetry Foundation in 2003, and his pamphlet *19th Century Blues* was a winner in the 2006 Poetry Business Competition. His books for Carcanet include his poetry collection *The Canals of Mars* (2004) and a translation of Stéphane Mallarmé's *For Anatole's Tomb*, as well as editions of T.E. Hulme's *Selected Writings* (1998), and the poetry and prose of Lynette Roberts (2005, 2008).

As well as writing and editing several academic books, he has presented programmes for radio, including the Sunday Features *A Short History of Stupidity* and *The Art of Idleness* for Radio Three. His first novel, *The Last Hundred Days*, is about the final months of Communism in Romania.

Patrick McGuinness is Professor of French and Comparative Literature at St Anne's College, Oxford, and in 2009 was made Chevalier dans l'Ordre des Palmes académiques for services to French culture.

Also by Patrick McGuinness

Poetry
The Canals of Mars
19th Century Blues

As editor
T.E. Hulme: Selected Writings
Lynette Roberts: Collected Poems
Lynette Roberts: Diaries, Letters and Recollections

As translator
Stéphane Mallarmé: For Anatole's Tomb

PATRICK McGUINNESS

Jilted City

CARCANET

First published in Great Britain in 2010 by
Carcanet Press Limited
Alliance House
Cross Street
Manchester M2 7AQ

A CIP catalogue record for this book is available from the British Library
ISBN 978 1 85754 968 3

The publisher acknowledges financial assistance from Arts Council England

Typeset by XL Publishing Services, Tiverton
Printed and bound in England by SRP Ltd, Exeter

O mémoire, cité trahie

'O memory, jilted city'

Henri Thomas

In memory of my mother

Acknowledgements

Many of these poems appeared first in the following magazines: *Agenda*, *Alhambra Poetry Calendar*, *Archipelago*, *The London Review of Books*, *Planet*, *PN Review*, *The Times Literary Supplement* and *The Yellow Nib*; and in the following books or anthologies: *From the Small Back Room: A Festschrift for Ciaran Carson*, edited by W.R. Irvine (Netherlea, Belfast, 2008), *Branchlines: Edward Thomas and Contemporary Poetry*, edited by Lucy Newlyn and Guy Cuthbertson (Enitharmon, 2007), *The European Constitution in Verse* edited by David Van Reybrouck and Peter Vermeesch (Passaporta, Brussels, 2009) and *Identity Parade: Contemporary British and Irish Poetry*, edited by Roddy Lumsden (Bloodaxe, 2010).

'Déja-vu' appeared as a Treganna Press poetry card, with a cover image by Alun Hemming, whose 'Urban Vulture' provides the cover for this book.

Several of these poems also appeared in the pamphlet *19th Century Blues*, which was a winner in the Poetry Business competition in 2006 and published by Smith Doorstop in 2007. I am grateful to Peter Sansom and The Poetry Business for permission to reprint it here. A broadsheet entitled *Montreal and Other Poems* appeared in the San Marco Press Five Poets series in 2006, with an Italian version of the title poem by Barbara del Mercado.

The sequence 'Blue Guide' also appears in French, in a version by Gilles Ortlieb, in the review *Théodore Balmoral*.

I am extremely grateful to Jennie Feldman for letting me use her inspired rendering of the line from Henri Thomas's poem 'Audides' as the epigraph to this book, and letting me have 'Jilted City' as the title. The rest of the poem can be found in *Into the Deep Street: Seven Modern French Poets 1938–2008*, edited and translated by Jennie Feldman and Stephen Romer (Anvil, 2009).

Contents

I

II Blue Guide

III

I

Déjà-vu

Two tenses grappling with one instant, one perception:
forgotten as it happens, recalled before it has begun.

Blue

Azur! Azur! Azur! Azur!
                                    Mallarmé

in memory of Malcom Bowie

Azure! Azure! Azure! Azure!... all that was before:
before we rode it in planes or used it to park satellites,
or as ethereal landfill for our emissions. All the best skies

these days are polluted: jet-fuel-refracted intricacies
of dead air and carbon-dazzle, cyanose confetti
that we mistake for light as we mistake mirrors

for what they show us of ourselves. But the thought
of all that emptiness, its promise of fresh starts, persists...
and though aftermaths look much the same

we never think of them as happening in the sky.
We never think of them as *starting* in the sky:
only beginnings are possible in such virgin air,

we think, harvesting new breath from frictionless
blue fields, those oxygen plantations with their Boeing
ploughlines and their furrows of weightless tilth.

But each square of it is Heathrow or JFK, tailbacks
of landing lights, control-tower static, log-jams of conditioned
air and shredded cumulus. First breath, first light: the original

repetitions, and the sun all the more intricate in its dying back
for the furnace it was at the beginning. And it's beginnings
that we dream of as we observe the blue, the great illusion

that every day it starts again, from zero, that perfect world-
shaped formula for all or nothing: *O*

The Age of the Empty Chair

In Monet's *The Beach at Trouville*, it is week one of the
                                        Franco-Prussian war.
The chair lodges in the sand between two women. One reads, the
                                        other

points her face at the emptying beach. The chair belongs to no one,
it is a found chair, a *trouvaille*, and there is never one chair too many

but one sitter too few. A flag rigid on its pole indicates
a swelling in the air, or something stronger, and the rent waves,

delicate turmoils of spume and lace, are distant cousins of the
                                        revolution
bound into the ebb and flow it breaks free of, then breaks back into.

There is sand in the paint; the place is mixed into its making
and even the brushstrokes replicate the water's peaks as they take

the light: roofs pell-mell across a city skyline, flashpoints in the sun.
The chair suggests all that can be suggested about change, but it
                                        remains

apart from it: the way a sail suggests the wind, the way a shell holds
a recording of the waves even as the waves turn around it.

Noon at the DoubleTree Hotel

for Christopher Ricks

From here the river looks like a road
surprised by its own keen swerve, the boaters
stitching the water's skin as above them a Boeing
rends the sky and the sky heals over.

It's all inaudible through the triple-
glazed panes, but by something in that improbable
clear blue we know it's heavy with noise,
drenched in spent jet fuel,

and the bright blue emptiness
is emptiness only, a desert of burned-off ozone
where the sun's ferocious waste scatters
its perfect, equalising light.

Shadows straighten up, level
with the shapes that threw them – house, high-rise,
Hummer – then disappear; and for a moment
all is its original, unencumbered self.

The clock's hands cross.
The two halves of the day come face to face.
The grainy, detailed hours have reached their zenith,
now they fall away.

The Shape of Nothing Happening

Dust knows the places we have forgotten, or we never see,
marking out the margins of our world: the window ledge's
cracked paint, the bevelled edges of a door frame,
the dado rails, the skirting boards, stifling the emphatic

corners of our lives. It fills the gulf behind the sofa,
that small domestic void that stands for losing and forgetting,
or for finding once again. It stands for things
that outlive their necessity; for us busily outliving

ours – particles slow dancing in a shaft of light
shedding the excess that each day we renew.
Its tininess is a feat of scale, but it cannot disappear.
It is the shape of nothing, the shape of nothing happening,

and of nothing's impossibility; matter worrying away
at trying not to be, and being all the while; reminding us
there are no absolutes, that all is graded on the scale,
that all is incremental, deciduous, and undecided.

French

Teaching it to my children I think of it now as my mother's
tongue if not, any more, my mother-tongue. It's freighted
with a kind of loss; hers, mine, and what she lost as she passed
it on to me, continents away from where she started:
shot through with gaps, mothballed and moth-
eaten at once, the smell of preservation neck and neck
with the smell of death. Lying for years in the cellar,
it fattened up, grew milky, slow, echoed in my mouth
as in a tunnel of its own disuse.
                              Then, like drinking
from the source, came our annual summers in Bouillon,
where our Belgitude rose up in us like the damp
behind the wallpaper in the house that stayed unused
nine months out of twelve: its empty rooms,
lost cupboards, the stored-up junk piled up so long
that each forgotten item now dovetailed into the next,
a perfect carpentry of abandonment; it was the tongue
and groove of unused words, life in suspension, ready to rise
again like dust in the backdraft from a closing door.

There's something in it when I use it here brings back
those moments when, mid-play, I'd nip indoors for a piss
or for a sandwich and when I came back out the other
children were all gone, the courtyard empty, the toys
back in their boxes and the sky already crossed with evening;
brings back the knowledge, always wrong but always knowledge,
that there would never be another time than this,
this ending-tainted perpetuity.

                              Now my children taste it,
the empty-courtyard French I used to speak;
they push their tongues along the language
and as I hear their words snag I hear my own again
and wake from that recurrent dream in which
I'm always waking up, and break off that aborted
first line of my story which I'm always starting:
that I'm much younger and still Belgian.

Le Grand Pardon

after notes by Rilke

We talk, but what do we know?
Somewhere the Angel of Oblivion,
radiant, leans his face into the wind
that turns our pages.

[Untitled]

after notes by Rilke

As Venetian glass
from the moment it is born
knows this shade of grey
the uncertain light that catches it

so your gentle hands
knew in advance
they were the scales that weighed
the fullest of our hours.

The Companions

You see us in the margins of their photographs, then in the margins
of their wills: governesses in our purgatory of *déclassement*,
somewhere between the housekeeper and the family doctor.

We speak in sentences from *Poirot*, teashop English; we speak
the language of the listener, the tilted ear and the bitten tongue;
we've digested our pride and swallowed all the manuals:

deportment, conversation, how to eat keenly but without
famishment, sceptically though without distaste. Our deferential
patter is always at the ready, balanced between talking in depth

and having no view, or changing opinion as a sail tacks back
on itself, unresisting but always using what's against it to pull by.
Those photographs you see us in, group portraits where we look

down or look away, that smear of darkness in our laps
where our hands fidget with the shadow of our hat-brims
and our wombs plot the emptiness to come...

that's what it's like all day: the boys in sailor suits are always
blurred behind us, the white cells fill their veins like mist on rolls
                                                            of film,
and the girls are moulded from boredom and warm milk

and bleed alone in corners, which is how their parents
can tell them from their dolls. At night we sit alone
in attic bedsits and eat formaldehyde soup with swabs

of bread, then tuck ourselves up in bed like mummies,
embalmed with all our few possessions, sheets
wrapped around our open mouths, cheeks tight

around the silent scream they'll block their ears to
when they unravel us, our perfect skin intact, as nearly-new
as the day their drawing-rooms gave birth to us.

Nineteenth-Century Blues

Those were the days, though not for those who lived them.

Flaubert's people were at the heart of things,
the eye of the nineteenth century's storm.

Still it passed them by:

★

Fresh from slipping the Maréchale one Frédéric returns
to the woman who, though she does not know it,
lives only inside his head.

Even to herself she is no more than half-there,
however totally described.

The language enfolds her. Later it embalms her.

★

The men are rudderless, bobbing like those balloons
that overflew the siege of Paris:
they roll on frictionless, leaving holes in the air.

Minnows caught in the slipstreams of their own stories,
they tremble for a moment upcurrrent, then are gone
into the next instalment, the next word.

Charleville

It's not why Rimbaud left that mystifies, though this New Year
the Place Ducale sports ice rink, carousel, and a *waffel*-stand
From nearby Belgium. It's why he kept returning. *On ne part pas*:
he answered himself, *You never leave.* After Harar,

he thought his hometown was a desert by other means,
and everywhere he walked he walked on sand – sinking
and finding his footing were the same. The sober *bateaux-*
mouches grazed on absinthe-coloured algae while barges

slid through bilgewater with rooftile cargoes
of *Ardennes ardoise*: slates bound into sheaves,
books with blackboard pages and all the boats
were floating libraries and all the letters spelled *azure*

or, after rain, *erasure,* which soon became its synonym.
Now his name is on every shopfront, from the obvious –
Le Rimbaud bookshop or *café-tabac* – to the genuinely
promising: the Rimbaud shoeshop, specialist in ripped soles

and the Opticien Rimbaud who tests your eyes with mirages
and rights near-sightedness with prescription telescopes.
Follow in his footsteps, the brochure offers, each one a wingbeat on
                                               the air,
the muscle of glass under water: heel-flash, frayed hem,

butt-ends and sand in the turn-ups, and for a moment the fashion
boutique dummies model louse-ridden jackets and half-mast trousers
with pockets flipped out like limp dicks. *Le Look Rimbaud!*
violet rays of neon stage-whisper to the forgetful night.

Black Box

Every crashed marriage has its black box, the blow-
by-blow account of what went wrong and how,
the crescendo of mistakes that peaks, is for an instant
quiet on its crest of trauma, then drowns itself and us

in a cascade of static. The black box is what survives;
anthracite gleaming in the wreckage where, preserved in anger,
the voices that it holds replay their lifetime of last moments
and speak of how, until the very end, it might all have been

so different; and how, right from the start, they knew it never would.

II
Blue Guide

I *Gare du Nord*

Arriving is like walking in on someone else's divorce
proceedings: Belgium-wide, the Balkans, their weather,
their slowly fissuring statelets ripening into crisis,
averted crisis, crisis. There are no last straws;
that's a law we Belgians learned too late; some of us

not at all. The rain falling slantwise over Gare du Nord:
Brussels composing its island weather, *Symphony
in grey major*, the nineteenth century still shaking
on the rails, the twentieth a late train.

II *Gare centrale*

I had it for a moment, quick as the clash of two winds on a rooftop:
the smell of barley, hops, fresh diesel and its negative – used air;
then *Belga* smoke over the exhalations of the *waffel*-stand:

*This feeling of penetrating misery is sponsored by Brussels
City Council in association with SNCB* announced a voice
in white over the station tannoy. I filed this one away between

two stops, between Bruxelles-Nord and Bruxelles-
Midi, between the word *départ*, so definitive and final,
and the word *partance*, an ongoing going, a leaving

still entangled in itself years later like the sound of a train
turning the corner, its siren coiled around the echo of the last to go
and the tunnel taking a moulding of our departures.

III *Gare du Midi*

Noon, the day's South Pole. On separate trains again:
window to window, each of us learns our sense
of movement from the way the other pulls away.

IV *Quartier-Léopold*

Colonial moss and plumes of baroque fern...
a station like a mouldy cake layered for a forgotten
coronation: icing stucco, pillars of sponge,

then a heart of darkness where the train stops,
a spasm in the network: the doors stay closed,
and the windows bead with tropical damp.

A moment in the striplit shadows, *Gare de Léopoldville*,
then we ease back into Belgium, a barge
sliding through diamond-studded blood and water.

V *Schuman*

(The other Robert Schuman, one *n*, this one
so anonymous they named a station after him
where it's dark enough to cultivate endives,

breed bats and harvest mushrooms,
where the only music is piped like chloroform
from unseen speakers into Euroland's conditioned air.)

VI *Bruxelles-Luxembourg*

Something is taking shape, a Leviathan fattened on damp
and disregard: the bureaucratic Unconscious, with its pagers,
mobile phones and trouserpresses, taking all our deepest

desires and fears, our primal hatreds and our hardest drives,
and making them fill in forms. A new language which has no name
spreads along the billboards and the shopsigns – *Euro Dago*,

Le YES Bar, Het Leader Bowling – beside which the sign marked
Liquidation totale seems full of Old Testament promise. Caught
on the down-bound escalator the one time in my life I stopped here:

the funereal blush of marzipan fruit in the *chocolatier*'s window,
laid out in their crinkled doilies like Lenin in his mausoleum,
and the ghost of their taste in my mouth: sugar dipped in
                                                    formaldehyde.

VII *Ottignies**

Asking myself, for the thousandth time, how such a one-
horse town can be the only stop whose name comes as a plural.

[*change here for Louvain-la-Neuve, a station with a Delvaux mural
of another station, to whose night-time departures and arrivals
your own journey is the mural.]

VIII *Gembloux*

As in: the father and son, picnicking against the wind turbine,
the wheels still idly turning on their bicycles, look a little *gembloux*
to me, at any rate from this distance and through this glass

and past the frosted letters designating the *sortie de secours*:
Don Quixote and Sancho Panza tilting at windfarms whose bright
white trunks rise like steamer chimneys in a sea of maize.

They turn in synch but there's no breeze; each one plugged
into the national grid to make us think the wind still blows.

Correspondances

The half-hour standstill between Poix-Saint-Hubert
and somewhere else whose name you've never caught
despite forty years of passing it and a little less
of thinking yourself attentive to all that passes you
is time in bas-relief, emphatic in its hollowness:
a rising tide of empty minutes draining
all the station clocks from here to Arlon,

their blank faces hung like moons above the platforms
where sheets of tabulated time contrive to be at once
exact (the 11.27 to Namur)
and untrue (it isn't there).
                Correspondances
is what they call connecting trains, even when

they don't connect. Even when they don't exist.
But as in Baudelaire's poem, the page
is where they couple, that hub of all encounters,
the clearing in the forest of iron and steam.

IX *Namur*

The station pigeon in his grey coat and his human half-rhyme
the station tramp are dressed identically: one patrols the guano-
lacquered buttresses, the other eyes the pigeon-proof netting

like a grounded acrobat hating the safety net that broke his fall.
Our longest scheduled stop. All the lines meet here,
and pass through: at Ostende wet sand clogs the hourglass;

in Bertrix the talk is of suicide, slate and rain,
where the track is ballasted with broken rooftiles
and a fog rises off the tepid, unemphatic hills.

The next start: a tug at the engine end, the carriages aligned,
setting like broken bones as the Porte de Namur,
a café on the edge of town you failed to notice coming in,

now appears as an after-image etched in light
against the glass, then against your eyelid
as you try to blink it off: Namur opening as it sweeps

from view – quayside, citadel, river-coloured sky
all widening like a dynamited gorge as you head into
la wallonnie profonde, deepest Wallonia,

and if you ask how a country that takes an hour
and a half to cross can have such a thing as *depth*
the rain against the window will remind you

how six inches of water is enough to drown in.
Liquidation totale. The train pulls out to a rumble
of dislodgement, the grince of wheels – resistance

turning to momentum – then a small silence long enough
to frame, as completely as the black rubber frames
the wall of cloud against the glass, the clack of a *pétanque*

ball followed at a distance by its clipped gravel splash.

X *Ciney*

The pines yeasting up in the shade they make along the tracks,
and suddenly the brewery sign rears up: a half-raised glass half-full.

XI *Marloie*

The platforms here are higher than the trains,
so that stepping in is like entering a moving cellar
or the cabin of a fishing boat, nose to nose

with the dockside and its smells. People's shoes,
the turn-ups of their trousers, army boots,
the liquorice wheels on rolling suitcases,

then Marloie, which you never saw,
gone in the beat of a newspaper's wing.

XII *Jemelle*

The station halves the town: on one side a Funerarium
beside a shop that sells *Variétés* (of what?),
and on the other the old station standing at our back,

a haunting in red brick with smoke effects of brick dust.
Then the industrial-sized rose window in the apse
of the engine shed that's tagged with graffiti and levitates

on a cushion of dry grass. Freight carriages rust
to an autumn-coloured powder, their iron fine
as gold plate, their wheels trellises for weeds to climb

in circles. One, half-way up the hill, has that shot-
while-escaping look of a boat dragged onto land
along a pair of rails that just gives up, not

suddenly, dramatically, but in increments
of disappearance like lifeboat tracks dissolving
in the surf. The telephone poles along the platform

beat out their twenty-metre intervals and each time
cut across the station name: first *Je* then *elle*,
more than twenty metres between them now, between us,

each in our neutral, barely even melancholy place.

XIII   *Libramont*

That *libre* you think you hear in *Libramont*
lasts no longer than it takes you to work out the sign
marked *Toutes directions* is an exaggeration.

XIV *Bouillon*

No train has stopped here since the 50s, but it remains
in all the ways that count my stop. It still says *Gare*
above the arch, the *guichet*'s glass has stayed unbroken,

the tracks are gone but there's a kind of stitching
in the ground, parallel scars where grass shrinks
back from growing. Then, kerbside vertigo:

that two-foot drop from platform-edge into
the next arrival, its endlessly suspended service,
and a few (never so aptly named as here, now)

railway sleepers, hold all I've ever known, in miniature,
of the world's speed and its solidity, a delirium of lost
footing followed by the knowledge that there was nowhere

further I could fall. This is still the *quartier de la gare*,
where the rain comes down like credits on an old film,
a roll-call of lost professions: slate-cutter, gamekeeper,

sommelier, market-gardener, butcher's boy, seamstress,
blacksmith, breeder of rabbits and dole queue *flâneur*...
the last being my grandfather, tempering each day to a fine point

on the soft anvil of his idleness. *Artisan du temps libre*
he called himself, *artisan of the empty hours*:
filling his days of worklessness in the Café de la Gare,

then hollowing out his nights in the Hôtel de la Gare;
he never made his mark on anything and yet I see him everywhere.

XV *Marbehan*

1 – *the way in*

Disappointed that the place has given me nothing, even in its
passing, to write a line about, I am gifted (along with the disap-
pointment, which I do not waste) the window of the
waiting-room that commemorates – 1895–1980 – Maurice
Grevisse, the great French grammarian; or rather, to disambiguate,
the great Belgian grammarian of French, here in his home town
called 'Monsieur Bon Usage', Marbehan's *Mr Grammar*, and
immortalised in the waiting-room of language.

2 – *the way out*

The houses in a domino effect of turned backs
show us their gardens as we leave town:
children's trampolines, basketball
gibbets and the fervent, verdurous algae

in the paddling pool where a deflated ball
puts me in mind of Monet's waterlilies at Giverny,
scattered with flakes of sun. Then nothing.

Sky, its blue non-sequitur.
Two minutes. Now clothespegs on a line:
quotation marks around an empty afternoon.

XVI *Arlon*

Pricking my thumb with the corner
of the passport I've never had to show

(the old black hardback with the window for your name,
not the new EU version with the rounded edge
and the silver-mauve pages like the lining of a raincloud
eviscerated by a blade of sun)

was always the sharpest sensation of the journey.

Kleinbettingen

Not quite a stop but neither are we merely passing through –
a kind of sticky pause like fighting a magnetic field
and wanting it to win. A few kilometres across the border,

the change in language comes like a switch in current,
a switch in currency. Here too the old station,
fresh from an antique postcard and all in sepia-tone,

keeps watch over shunted carriages, slate wagons,
and a brace of NATO tanks. An infinity of sidings
deepens the perspective towards their vanishing point:

a motorway scything through bright fields of rape.

XVII *Luxembourg*

First, lunch on the Place d'Armes surrounded by men in vests
with small angry dogs, also in vests – one who looks like Churchill,
balls bullet-hard and straining at their sack; another, a poodle
in paramilitary fatigues, a face like Milošević, all bite –

           then back to a flat on Place de Paris,
so close to the station you can hear yourself miss the trains.

Stations where the train doesn't stop

Etterbeek, la Hulpe, Epinal, Rixensart, Profondsart,
Mont-Saint-Guibert, Ernage, Lonzée, Assesse, Aye,
Forrières, Grupont, Poix-Saint-Hubert, Habay, Viville,

a rosary of Belgian stations and their names,
all branchlines, sidings, or surviving as high-
watermarks of towns that have retreated
to a blur of white lettering on blue enamel.

III

My Mother

How I think about her now is how
a thought is said to cross the mind:
like a bird's shadow as it flies,
dragging its span in darkness along the ground.

L'Air du Temps

Tracing her perfume, link by link of vapour,
through the crowd to where she's not, to where
her scent expends itself in air
I pass through as if the ghost was me, not her.

The Other Side

*...that eventless realm, neither cold nor hot, neither hilly nor flat,
where the dead, each at their own best age and marooned in an eternal afternoon,
pass the ages with sod all going on.*

Hilary Mantel, *Beyond Black*

The dead flit lightly by. They have no ballast,
nothing can keep them down. Slowly,
like Zeppelins on the horizon, or thoughts
coming into view, they go about our lives.

Death has not altered their priorities.
They keep things in perspective.
They are as down to earth as ever,
shop locally, mow their universal lawns.

Around them a civil breeze of trespass
rustles in the trees, bends the flowers
in their flowerbeds, pries their shutters
open as the darkness rolls in from our day.

But they are not nostalgic. 'Life goes on'
they seem to say – 'all is much the same:
Eternity is just a small town age
and Night a darker shade of beige.'

Montréal

The letters on the Departures Board
are falling back into themselves: London
into Montreal via three brisk ripples
of the alphabet, Amsterdam, and six hours
in the air.

       Six hours later, on the Arrivals Board,
the letters are falling back into themselves:
Montreal collapses into London and returns
as *Montréal*; as if the French passed through
a fording of the English to find itself more French.

Daytime Drinking

First sip: gentle as a stream overreaching,
supple as a rope-bridge in the air;

The second, long as the creak of floorboards,
firm as a leg-iron clasp;

The third, sudden as the trap door beneath you,
the rudderless slide back to thirst.

Lists

for Sarah

I

Those last few weeks were in a way the first;
at any rate, the first we'd really got along:
three decades' tension, stretched and racked across
our adolescence, his short life's lifelong
disappointment…

    but there was hardly time;
for us to make our peace with him, for him
to make peace with himself; though there was always
plenty for regret, recrimination, for things
that took time from us and gave nothing back.

II

One day he made a list of all the things
he was sorry he'd never do again.
Most of them he'd never done at all; the rest
he'd never liked in any case. But dying
does that, knowing that the light at the end
of the white foreshortened corridor
is not the world outside, but something
outside the world.

    Then the walks along the ward,
looking for those worse off, someone to feel
better than; short walks on shortening breaths,
as he drowned in his own lungs, to the last self-
consumed.

    The cancer spread like fury,
the way his anger would take hold,
would fill his lungs, the house, our lives.

III

Unlovable as ever, yet he was brave,
with that aura of unshared suffering
that spared us everything but grief
at knowing what we felt was not exactly grief.

IV

His skin like paper, that first X-ray was his watermark;
the shadow he had cast, he now cast inside himself:

death's stamp, grey against the window,
daylight burned away by one dark star.

V

Even now, even at the end, it was better left unspoken.
All my anger decompressed in those last weeks,

because I knew they were the last. I was lost
without it; he lost at no longer finding it in me.

VI

You'd recall:
his refusal to cave in to optimism,
the palliatives of mind and body
that would just extend the run-up to the night.

And I:
how easily he let it go, his life of graft
and grudging drudgery, the days racked

up on his mind's prison wall, *tomorrow*
and tomorrow and tomorrow...

but that last day there was only one.
Then nothing. None.

Spleen: Cardiff Matchday Blues

some way after Baudelaire

These arcades are no Arcadia; steel glades
whose girdered glass matches the angle of the rain;
matches, too, its colour – the colour of pigeons,
tanks, the dishwater sluicing the drains

as the streets gargle their litter.
There's a shop closed on every corner.
There's a shop cloned on every corner.
In all the papers, deficit, terror, loss,

and at home, deficit, terror, loss.
Plastic bags ride the wind in torn surrender.
Here it is always half-time, where the stopped
clock gets it right
                    pretty much all day.

The Thaw

a sequence of dispoetry after Christian Dotremont

I *Illegible waves of wood*

The wood's illegible waves on the desk
as you write. The first principle of form:
the wave, rings of a dropped stone.

A ridge of water, muscle stretching
in spreading circles,
gathering in what lies around,

gathering up the stream it is part of.
So the rings of a tree: the tree ages,
thickens into the space around;

marks its past concentrically.
It remembers itself: flesh over flesh,
core hardening to rind,

becoming its own record.
Drawing in the years to lay them
side by side in space, in time.

II *Lapland*

The trees are exclamation marks,
the snow a long white knotted cry.

A forest of geometry,
each flake locked into its neighbour;

a polar hive, walls flush as well-
laid bricks. Each minute of the day

in place: the eye, round as the world,

sees in waves: fractals, pixels, jpeg,
the plasma screen. White busy against white.

III *! ! !*

Sleighs harvest the silence.
The cabins breathe in/breathe out.

The boats are flying in upended sky,
icebreakers clean their beaks on clouds of rye.

The hiss and suck of the thaw
angles becoming curves, diamonds becoming tears.

IV *Stills*

The bubbles rise like stitches in the glass:
threading the spirit to the body,
winding the water round the wine.

Fire and ice, ice and fire:
take away the bottle and the drink still stands,
shoulders braced against the air.

V *writing the words*

…as they move along the page
the virtual/
the vellum, cursor skimming
the blue ripples of the laptop;

the quill slides,
the electric ink of its wake.

Disks glint, stacked in their archives
of ice. The paper dreams of the wood,
the grain implicit beneath
– between – its skin.

VI *L O! v e*

Return journey to the void
via plenitude.
My bad luck. Nobody gets off here
but me.
The fourteenth station.

I love you historically
who gave me everything you had
save nothing.

i.m. Jacques Brel (1929–1978)

He was always there, tramping the wet
pavements of his heart, the streets he said pissed
in both the languages he wept in.

He riffled the pages of his A to Z
of grief: from Amsterdam to Zangra,
via the Casino d'Ostende and the Mort Subite.

That concert in l'Olympia he knelt and supplicated
ten thousand people as if he were an empty station
and they the departing train. He danced

his last tango on the promenade of Knokke-le-Zoute:
the man of La Mancha, the man of La Manche –
the Don, but Juan or Quixote?

Article 0.5: The Right to Be In-Between

from 'The European Constitution in Verse'

This article enshrines inalienably the right to alienation
for those who want it: Republicans of the in-between,
celebrants of the glorious prefix *trans* and all its panoply
of cognates, cousins, second cousins, siblings, half-siblings,
in-laws and out-: the *neither/nor*, the *both/and*, the *none
of the above*, the signatories of the dotted sideline,
citizens of the hard-shoulder, the *terrain vague*,
the inside-out and outside-in, the bi-, the semi-, the demi-
the ambi-, the half-blood, the half-caste, the rainbow-shades
of grey, the *entre-deux-guerres* and the *entre-deux-mers*,
the slipstream and the tributary, the river that changes its name,
the visa that's all in the vista and the port that's all in the passing.

Poem in White Ink

for Osian and Mari

Happiness writes white. It doesn't show on the page.
Maeterlinck

The Empty Frame

after a painting by Evan Walters

It's a photocopy of a printout of a photograph, now lost,
of a painting now destroyed. Step by step
we might think of it as progressively less there
the closer it comes to us, or of ourselves less

as seeing it here, on this page now, than as following
the story of its disappearance;
but here it is, intact and yet all ghost as well:
an empty frame propped up against a studio wall,

that interrupts the skirting board, the wallpaper,
that makes each flaw it finds into a pattern and each pattern
into a flaw: the bloom of musty damp along the wall
becomes Bohemia's famous coast, miles of motorway

hard shoulder, or a frontier complete with watchtowers
and flags, barbed wire, guards and dogs.
A window into, a window out from, it is the frame
that makes the picture, the way the margin makes the centre:

the squared-off angle, the spirit-levelled, bevelled
edge that marks the end of seeing, calls time on the eye,
that marks the border between the over-
and the unexamined life.

House Clearance

Turn the key: note how the emptiness accumulates
as you come in; how by being here at all you seem to add to it,

until it fills the corridor with that fermented stasis
you both disturb and add to as you move. Pass

through a second door, a portal of stirred air,
ignore the rooms to left and right and take the stairs,

your shoes dislodging dust that billows
up in tiny detonations. You're walking underwater,

the silt explodes beneath your feet; at first you think you'll drown
but what's flashing through your mind in one

slow-motion scattering of greys is not your own life but theirs.
No matter that you still can't breathe – that's how it's always

been in here: even the nothingness is thick as blotting paper
on which their shapes have spread like ink – must, damp,

the outline of a body sketched in mothballs and almost-
memory. The furniture is ghostly beneath the sheets

but the missing pictures are still there, outlined
in frames of dirt on squares of wall now white as bone

surprised beneath the skin. You were in every one of them.
Now you're the last flame in the grate:
Hamlet in his theatre of shadows, their embers at your feet.

The Clamour

The clamour is always just a thought away,
one wrong turning of the mind. I hear the cries
(they're mine) at the foot of a stair,
the end of a supermarket aisle,

and then it washes over in a tide of loss. All
gives way to chaos, or to what is always there:
that locked-out self that treads its mill of grief
waiting for her dying to die down.

Déjà-vu

Forgotten as it happens, recalled before it has begun:
two tenses grappling with one instant, one perception.

IV

City of Lost Walks
Poems by Liviu Campanu

Liviu Campanu (1932–1994) was a poet and university lecturer from Bucharest who fell out of favour with the Ceauşescu regime. After writing poems about the demolition of old Bucharest, Campanu was expelled from the Union of Writers and accused of being a 'reactionary nostalgist'. He was sacked from his post at the University of Bucharest and sent in 1984 to run a workers' education centre in Constanţa, the Black Sea town that, under its Roman name of Tomis, hosted Ovid's years of banishment. Campanu's small but unified poetic *oeuvre* consists of regretful meditations on place and placelessness, and on a particular kind of precarious tedium that characterises intellectual life in a totalitarian state.

Though he was never arrested and was no worse off materially than many of his compatriots who endured the hardships of the Ceausescu years, Campanu's travel was restricted and he was prevented from leaving Constanţa. No longer a member of the Union of Writers, he was excluded from the literary and cultural magazines, though still occasionally referred to by official critics. One such critic called Campanu's poems 'minor-key variations on a bourgeois Ovid complex', a phrase Campanu liked so much he used it as the title for one of the three chapbooks he privately printed and distributed among friends. Along with these, his collected works consist of one book which appeared from the state publishing house in 1976 (a time of relative cultural openness in Romania), and a further file of poems and notes that was found after his death. Campanu's intention was to collect these and the chapbooks into one volume, to be called *City of Lost Walks*, an allusion to the destruction of the old Bucharest he never returned to, even when he was allowed to do so.

After the fall of Ceauşescu in 1989, which, according to one baffled critic, 'his poetry fails to register except in the form of an omission so shocking that it quite overwhelms the work', Campanu was offered his old job and a seat on the board of Romania's most important literary review. For reasons still unclear, he refused this offer and stayed in Constanţa until his death.

English-language readers should be told that the epigraph to Campanu's *The Ovid Complex* is from the Romanian philosopher Emil Cioran, himself an exile who made his home in France and wrote in French.

from *The Ovid Complex* (1989)

Exile, at the beginning, is felt as a schooling in vertigo
Cioran

I

'Vertigo'! 'Vertigo'?
What's vertiginous about it?
We all carry our provinces around inside us,
but there's no such thing as a portable metropolis.
In Constanţa now since last April, I've learned
two words to chill the heart: *here* and *now*.
I'd make a useless existentialist, but isn't that the point?
Reluctantly I'm *here*, *now*, all my elsewheres
banked in some police file in Bucharest
the city where informers roam and even the snowflakes
photograph you as they fall.
I test my weakness
against some idea of fortitude, my impatience
against the stoic or the socialist ideal...
and I'm happy enough to be found wanting,
or would be if I knew what it was I wanted.

II

The dogs, like us, doze one eye open,
the half-starved cats lope hieroglyphically
around the bins, assess our meagre surplus,
and are unimpressed.

The mud is sumptuous around my ankles
as I walk the oil-drum-scattered bay
of Tomis, Constanţa, where the last synagogue's
pogrom-lashed walls still give off the heat,
the hate, that scorched them forty years ago.

Drift is what we worship here:
on the cast iron shore
the sea is rolling its dice and the heron,
the only bird who can make flying look difficult,
hauls himself up on a ramp of wind
like a geriatric on his stairlift.

The moist air fits; the breeze,
tucking into my waist,
is like a tailor breathing at my back,
my elbow, the crook of my arm,
nipping the cloth to fit my every contour.

At least my discomfort is bespoke.

III

I'm not adapting. But what's worse
is that I'm getting used to it: I'm a bad version
from the classics, Ovid in translationese,
jazzed up with radio and TV
(albeit black and white and with just one channel),
unable to hit the right note without feeling
I'm borrowing from someone else's story.

And what I complain most about is that it's *not exactly*
suffering, *not quite* extremity, but rather fretting
at tedium's hem, picking myself apart remembering
those nights in Bucharest, or one night in particular,
when we stole a moment on the balcony,
adultery's hanging basket, at the Union of Writers
Festival of Progressive Literature:
she was the trellis and I the vine (which is a bourgeois
poet's way of saying I was all over her).

IV

Schooling in vertigo, you say? I'll admit that it sounds pithy.
But aphorism is the fool's revenge on the world's complexity.

V

My window frames a moving postcard of the sea,
edges it in black like someone's funeral announcement.

The wind thumbs through its dictionary of greys,
the sky, and out to sea the usual waves
come back on different tides. I notice all of it:
each variegation on the sepia theme is as different
to my eyes, as, when I first arrived, it looked the same.

I think of how, by some proportionality
of contraries, everything you notice displaces
its own weight in inattention:
in the end it's always what you missed
that haunts you.

VI   (1989)

The news from Bucharest is that the regime is crumbling
the way rocks on the shore erode – by seeming not to.

VII

Roofslate, coal-sand, woodlouse-casing-grey,
the grey of waves under afternoon-blue sky,
the grey of a seagull's underwing, of litter
rippling in the wind like hat ribbons
or petticoats in a Monet beach scene.
Squint for it: *mademoiselle* in her layered frock
elaborate as a patisserie from Capsia's...

No, it's all a mirage, it's only today's paper,
which is a mirage in its own way too,
crossing the square like tumbleweed:
pages of targets, Five Year Plans,
Trade Fair Specials and the new tractor
that will launch a thousand poems.
Perhaps, somewhere, a review of Campanu's
The Ovid Complex: his latest work to absorb
– to actually *sponge up* – the critic's disregard.

VIII

Morning – *late* morning, judging by the ripeness
of the bin juice whose wafts the breeze
brings to my open window: the postman
with his letters from Bucharest, still wet
from being steamed open, the invisible

fingerprints that crawl across your words to me,
Cilea, like the hands I imagine stroking you
as I wank slackly behind swollen curtains
to the smell of crabmeat and the sound
of patriotic songs three radio sets away.

Scenarios for Lovers and Magnets

Amant, lover, and *aimant,* magnet:
it was our favourite of the *faux amis*
we watched for as we learned French,
and the contexts where we might confuse
them were so beautiful we sought them out,
sat up and wrote them out: scenarios
for lovers and magnets.
              And of all of them
I liked this one best (at least I did
until it became our scenario too):
the iron filings raised from the tabletop
by love alone, fighting gravity, staying afloat
in defiance of their own weight and of the air
that wanted only to see them fall…

then falling back at last
when one of them drifts out of range
or someone, something, cuts the current.

from *City of Lost Walks* (1985)

from the 'Museums of Bucharest' sequence

In the Natural History Museum

Room by room, beads on a string of corridors,
the lights up ahead come on and those behind
go out. It is a metaphor for History, or what passes
for it around here. But what's easier to feel is the momentum
of depletion, the world subtracting from itself faster

than it can replenish. We're caught in a present
so invested in becoming that year on year, Five Year Plan
by Five Year Plan, it fails to happen, or at any rate to us.
We fiddle the figures, stretch the graphs,
tour the exhibits and pay our homages of inattention...

but nothing changes, as the old joke goes, *except the past*:
the past they're always reinventing, so that we need to climb
the moving walls of History, to stay one step ahead of it,
the way a surfer rides his wave, his carpet of sheer momentum.
As we walk the scribes are in their carrels, cooped up

like battery hens, chewing garlic bulbs and smoking *Carpati*,
typing up the latest version: *History, the Variorum Edition*,
where the margins give the best (perhaps the only) view.
The Museum of Natural History was our refuge from all that –
we spent hours there in the old days, though only minutes at a time –

after all, I asked her under my breath, our hands joined
at the knuckles, *how can a brachiosaur be political?*
Check his police file she answered, her face straight
as a loaded dice, her lips hidden by a plastic cup of ersatz
coffee. All around us, dinosaurs in interrupted poses,

jaws wired back in silent screams, their articulated backbones
like the staircases of Bucharest's ruined palaces, chipped
and here and there a slab short, a segment gone, pianos
with missing keys each as differently out of tune as their
melody stayed the same: Mass extinction in B Minor.

Around them lay the plaster ghosts of their own feet,
long-gone and striding to the end of Time or treading the plates
of learned books in libraries, archives, police files,
huddled in the man-made caves of species-death. *Stegosaurus's
police file* she laughed, just loud enough for everyone to hear

though there was no one else around and our most likely eaves
                                                          dropper,
Homo sapiens was still three rooms and forty thousand years away,
hunched over his witless grin, his birdbath mouth, stupid in the face
of what he doesn't understand but already learning to reduce
it all to what he does.
                    We hold hands

(my thumb on her wrist but it's my own pulse I'm checking)
and survey the whole static safari. She tells me about Cuvier
the greatest poet of them all, she says, the paleontologist
who could take a tooth and reconstruct the animal
around it, who made wholes from the smallest part,

who fleshed the bone and sealed the flesh with skin,
dreamed a species from a femur, named it
and made it breathe in our imaginations.
The next room. Light off. Lights on. *We're caught between
two darknesses*, she whispered, *the one ahead and the one behind...*

yet always somehow passing through them both, I thought,
and the shadow that crosses our neck like liquid night,
or is it the scythe's cold slice of moon?

In The Museum of Archaeology

Proust's theory, one we disbelieve
despite our lives' daily demonstration of its truth,
is that what survives of us
is what was least intended to go on after.

The museums know that, with their shelves
of fluent trivia: whole civilisations summoned up
by beaten gold that's finer than skin, shards
of pot whose brokenness now renders them unbreakable,

sky-blue glass blown by one whose breath survives only
in the bubbles that were caught there, sculpted now
as tiny voids around which our idea of life beads
because there's nothing to it but what holds it in:

a see-through brittle shell of light around what only
looks like nothing. It's the nearest *we*'ll get to pure form,
to seeing it I mean, to time without the clock,
the river without the bank, that point when either

all is form or there's no such thing; in other words,
when form is most itself, both essence and tautology.
Proust knew it, whose every microsmos of a sentence
could have stood alone, the novel's DNA, the pinhead-dance

of all the world's complexity and ours in face of it;
and yet who needed the whole three thousand pages too,
to build up what had to be reduced.

Notes

Blue Guide: The historic rail line between Brussels and Luxembourg, 'La ligne 162', was begun in 1846 and inaugurated in 1858 by the Grande Compagnie du Luxembourg, a group of British businessmen who originally planned a rail link to India starting with a continuous track from Ostende to Trieste. It began at Quartier-Léopold station, and took passengers to the Grand Duchy of Luxembourg via Namur, now the regional Walloon capital, and through the Ardennes, part of the territory known as 'Les Forêts' by the French revolutionary law of 14 Fructidor III (31 August 1795).

In May 2000, Quartier-Léopold, Europe's oldest railway station, was renamed Bruxelles-Luxembourg, and all but the building's façade was demolished to make way for an underground station serving the European Community quarter.

The line plays its small part in European history. Among those who used it were great exiles such as Victor Hugo and Victor Serge, escaping Communards, Rimbaud and Verlaine fleeing debt and legal action, advancing German troops in both world wars and then retreating German troops in both world wars. In May 1864, Baudelaire, then living in Brussels, took the train as far as Namur to visit the artist Félicien Rops. Attempting to return to Brussels, he boarded the 162 in the wrong direction and finished up in Luxembourg before turning around, thus completing the length of the journey twice over.

The 162 is both a local line, with some stops little more than ten minutes apart, and an international line, from which all of Europe is available. 'Blue Guide' is about no single journey but about hundreds of journeys taken since my childhood, and my memories of them. It is also about realising, on my first cross-European Inter-Rail trip in 1987, that the train that would take me to Germany, Italy, Yugoslavia and beyond was the same train my family had used for generations to commute the twenty minutes between Libramont and Arlon. All I had to do was stay on the train a little longer.

The Thaw: Christian Dotremont (1922–1979) was a Belgian poet and artist. He founded the Belgian Revolutionary Surrealist Circle, and in 1948 co-founded the CoBRA group of artists, which took its name from Copenhagen, Brussels, Amsterdam. He retained a lifelong fascination with 'nordicity', and lived for extended productive periods in Lapland. 'Dispoetry' is a translation of his term 'Dépoésie'. His complete poems are published by Mercure de France, with an introduction by Yves Bonnefoy.

Article 0.5: The Right to Be In-Between: 'The European Constitution in Verse' was a project by the Brussels Poetry Collective in response to the failure of the European Constitution. Fifty poets from across Europe, writing in dozens of official and non-official EU languages, were invited to submit articles in verse for the new constitution, which was launched with a performance at Passa Porta in Brussels in March 2009 and published as a book in the Cahiers Passa Porta series.